HIGH-TECH
OLYMPICS

Nick Hunter

Heinemann
LIBRARY

Chicago, Illinois

www.heinemannraintree.com
Visit our website to find out more information about Heinemann-Raintree books.

To order:

☎ Phone 888-454-2279

💻 Visit www.heinemannraintree.com to browse our catalog and order online.

Edited by Kate de Villiers and Laura Knowles
Designed by Richard Parker
Picture research by Liz Alexander
Production by Camilla Crask
Originated by Capstone Global Library Ltd
Printed and bound in China by CTPS

15 14 13 12
10 9 8 7 6 5 4 3 2

Library of Congress Cataloging-in-Publication Data
Hunter, Nick.
  High-tech Olympics / Nick Hunter.
    p. cm.—(The Olympics)
  Includes bibliographical references and index.
  ISBN 978-1-4109-4121-3 (hc)—ISBN 978-1-4109-4127-5 (pb)
1. Olympics. 2. Physical education and training. 3. Technological innovations. I. Title.
  GV721.5.H845 2012
  796.48—dc22   2010049494

Acknowledgments
We would like to thank the following for permission to reproduce photographs: Alamy p. **9** (© Russell Price); Corbis pp. **7** (© Zhang Yanhui/Xinhua Press), **8** (© Bettmann), **15** (© Liu Dawei/xh/Xinhua Press), **19** (© Serge Timacheff), **21** (© Mike Blake/Reuters), **23** (© Jerry Lampen/Reuters), **25** (© Gilbert Iundt; Jean-Yves Ruszniewski/TempSport), **27** (© Leonhard Foeger/Reuters); Getty Images pp. **5 top**, **5 bottom** (Mark Dadswell), **6** (Billy Stickland /Allsport), **13** (Simon Bruty/Sports Illustrated), **12** (Lars Baron), **16** (Clive Mason), **17** (Paul Gilham), **20** (Popperfoto), **22** (China Photos); Shutterstock p. **11** (© Monkey Business Images).

Cover photograph of training run for the Men's Alpine Skiing Downhill Sitting event reproduced with permission of Getty Images/Quinn Rooney.

Every effort has been made to contact copyright holders of material reproduced in this book. Any omissions will be rectified in subsequent printings if notice is given to the publisher.

Disclaimer
All the Internet addresses (URLs) given in this book were valid at the time of going to press. However, due to the dynamic nature of the Internet, some addresses may have changed, or sites may have changed or ceased to exist since publication. While the author and publisher regret any inconvenience this may cause readers, no responsibility for any such changes can be accepted by either the author or the publisher.

Contents

Some words are shown in bold, **like this**. You can find them in the glossary on page 30.

Olympic Dreams

In the Olympic **stadium**, three athletes stand on the medal **podium**. They wear medals around their necks: a bronze medal for the athlete who finished third, silver for second, and gold for the Olympic champion. The athletes have proved they are the best in the world.

Technology at the Olympics

Winning an Olympic medal requires skill and many years of training. Training and competing at the Olympics also depends on **technology**. In the 300 different Olympic events, from athletics to weightlifting, technology helps athletes to run faster, jump higher, and break records.

Technology is also important in bringing the world together for the Olympics. The first modern Olympics were held in Athens, Greece, in 1896. The only way of getting to Athens was by land or sea. In 2012, athletes from more than 200 nations will fly into London in the United Kingdom for the Olympics.

100 meters–then and now

The 100-meter race decides who is the fastest man or woman in the world. In 1896, Thomas Burke of the United States won in 12 seconds. In 2008, Jamaica's Usain Bolt won in 9.69 seconds. Part of the improvement in times is due to changes in technology such as **starting blocks**, athletes' clothing, and improved training methods.

The 100-meter sprint then and now. Athletes' clothing has changed a lot since 1896.

On the Track

Shoe **technology** is essential for runners. Englishman Joseph William Foster invented running spikes in the 1890s. Foster's "running pumps" included six one-inch spikes. Like modern running spikes, the shoes had no heel. Spikes are different depending on the distance the athlete is running. Spikes for sprinters are very light with no padding.

Australia's Cathy Freeman won 400-meter gold at the Sydney Olympics in 2000. Her suit allowed air to flow more easily over her body.

For many years, Olympic medals were won on dusty "cinder" tracks. Today's running tracks are made of rubber, designed to be springy without being soft. Many of the materials in London's Olympic track will be recycled. **Starting blocks** were first used at the 1928 Olympics. They prevent runners from slipping at the start. Before then, runners dug a little hole in the track.

Shoes are for wimps!

Although technology has helped athletes run faster, athletics is still about the contest between one athlete and another. The right shoes will only get you so far, as Ethiopia's Abebe Bikila proved when he won the 1960 Olympic **marathon** with bare feet!

OSCAR PISTORIUS (BORN 1986)

South African Oscar Pistorius, nicknamed the "blade runner," lost both his legs as a baby. He has won **Paralympic** titles running on **artificial** legs made of wood and **carbon fiber.** Pistorius plans to run in both the Paralympics and Olympics in 2012.

Jumping and Throwing

Some athletic events use **technology** as part of the sport. The pole vault would be no good without the pole that athletes use to jump over a high bar. Changes in materials have helped pole-vaulters jump much higher. In the early 1900s a solid wooden pole was used. Today's pole-vaulters use a **fiberglass** pole, which is very light and strong. It will bend more without snapping, to help athletes spring over the bar.

Dick Fosbury and the high jump

Before the Mexico City Olympics, high-jumpers landed in a sand pit. In 1968, a much softer landing mat was introduced. This helped American Dick Fosbury to win gold in the high jump by jumping backwards over the bar and landing head-first on the mat. Now every high-jumper does the "Fosbury Flop."

Going too far

One event uses technology to stop people from breaking records. Javelin throwers throw a pointed javelin as far as possible. The javelin has been an Olympic sport since the **ancient Olympics**, which began in Greece in 776 BCE. When athletes started throwing the javelin more than 100 meters, people worried that spectators could be in danger. The javelin design was changed, so that it could not be thrown so far.

Pole-vaulters, such as Yelena Isinbaeva of Russia, must have very strong shoulders to master this difficult event. Isinbaeva was Olympic champion in 2004 and 2008.

Training for the Top

At the first modern Olympics, most athletes had not really trained much. For any athlete wanting to win an Olympic medal in the 21st century, years of practice are essential. Science and **technology** are part of every athlete's training plan.

Sports science and medicine

When the modern Olympic Games started, little was known about the effects of sports on the body. Since then, sports science has increased understanding of how athletes should train, what they should eat, and how much rest they need.

Video can be used to review the performance of athletes and their rivals before and after competing. Electronic monitors track the effects of training on athletes' bodies. For many years, rowers have trained using ergometers (indoor rowing machines) to monitor their performance.

An athlete's diet

Eating the right food is essential for Olympic success. Athletes and trainers know much more about diet than they used to. An athlete's diet depends on their sport. Rowers use a lot of energy. They need a diet rich in **carbohydrates** and **proteins**, including foods such as wholegrain bread, lean meat, fish, fruit, and vegetables. An Olympic rower in training needs 6,000 **calories** per day. The average adult only needs about 2,000 calories per day.

As this athlete exercises on a treadmill, her doctor measures her heart rate. This is a good way to find out a person's level of fitness.

In the Pool

Swimming has been part of the Olympics since the first modern Games in 1896. The first Olympic swimming pool was built in London in 1908. Before then, swimming events took place in the ocean and in rivers.

The first Olympic swimmers wore heavy wool clothing. Wool becomes heavier when it gets wet, so it was gradually replaced by lighter materials. Swimsuits also got smaller. Australian Annette Kellerman, the first woman to wear a one-piece swimsuit with bare arms and legs, was arrested in 1907! The first bare-chested male swimmers did not appear at the Olympics until 1936.

Synchronized swimming

Technology affects all sports. Synchronized swimmers perform gymnastic routines to music in the pool. They use special nose clips to prevent water from going up their noses when they do upside-down movements underwater. They also have loudspeakers underwater so they can hear the music.

Michael Phelps has won more gold medals than anyone in Olympic history. His body suit meant that he and other swimmers were able to set faster times at the Beijing Olympics.

Super suits

At the 2008 Olympics in Beijing, China, most swimmers wore new all-over body suits. These suits were designed to help swimmers move more smoothly through the water. After 25 world records were broken in Beijing, the rules were changed to prevent people from wearing these suits.

On the Water

Many sports at the Olympics take place on water, including sailing, rowing, and canoeing. These sports rely on athletes getting the best out of the **technology** they are using.

Olympic sailors race each other in the same type of boat so that no one has an advantage. In the early 1900s, the boats were heavy and wooden with many people on board. Today's boats use lightweight, but strong, materials, such as **fiberglass**. Windsurfing has been an Olympic sport since 1984. Olympic sailors have to be fit and **agile** to balance their light boats against the power of the wind.

Formula One technology

Rowers, sailors, and cyclists do not travel as fast as a Formula One racing car, but they use the same technology to win Olympic gold. Formula One uses high-tech instruments to get information about driver and car performance. Olympic teams now use this technology to understand how to make boats and bicycles move faster.

Comfort and safety

Athletes competing in sailing and canoeing events can get very wet. Wetsuits have made life much more comfortable for them. Helmets and lifejackets are essential for safety during the white-water excitement of canoe slalom.

White water courses for canoe slalom are often specially designed and built for the Olympics.

On Your Bike

The bicycles in all four Olympic cycling events have two wheels and pedals. But the similarity ends there. The rest of each bike—and the skills needed to win a medal on it—are very different.

Road racing and track racing on an oval wooden track have been Olympic sports since 1896. The bicycles have changed a lot over time. Track bikes now use much lighter materials, such as **carbon fiber** frames. Parts of a normal bike, such as **gears** and brakes, are removed to cut **air resistance** and make the bike as light as possible. A modern track bike weighs around 14 pounds (7 kilograms).

Track racing bikes have no gears and no brakes.

Extended aerobars help the rider to get into a crouched position for less air resistance

Solid wheels give extra speed

Fixed gear with no freewheeling device means less weight on the bike

Mountain biking

Cross-country mountain biking was introduced for the 1996 Atlanta Olympics. Developments in **technology** made this sport possible. Tougher bikes with quick-change gears and **suspension** for a smoother ride meant that cyclists could go off-road. These cyclists are allowed to carry toolkits with them in case anything goes wrong.

Rough riding

BMX racing became an Olympic sport in 2008. The bikes are designed to be as tough as possible, to deal with the rough ground and jumps of the race. Wheels have many spokes so that they keep their shape. Like track racing, BMX bikes do not have gears.

Seconds and Milliseconds

Olympic athletes want to record the fastest time or the longest jump. **Technology** has helped to measure times and distances more and more precisely.

Accurate timing is very important in sprint or swimming events. Athletes may be separated by just one hundredth of a second. In the past, people measured times by pressing a stopwatch. Today, automatic electronic timing is used. Photographs can decide the winner in close finishes. When swimmers touch the pool wall at the end of their race, the clock stops.

Is it a hit?

Fencing has been a part of every modern Olympic Games. In this sport, athletes try to hit each other with blunted swords. Athletes are wired up electronically to the scoring system and hits are counted automatically. Before electronic scoring, a team of judges counted the hits. In the early 1900s, fencers wore black and had chalk on the ends of their swords, so hits would show up on their opponent's clothes.

False start

Starting blocks in sprint events are linked to a device that can tell if an athlete starts before the starting gun (a false start). If an athlete leaves the blocks less than 0.12 seconds after the gun is fired, it is called a false start, because the athlete could not react to the gun faster than that.

Fencing is an ancient sport. The first evidence of fencing comes from ancient Egypt more than 3,000 years ago.

Winter Olympic Technology

Timing is also essential for Winter Olympic sports such as bobsled and skiing, where athletes race one at a time against the clock. The Winter Olympics are held every four years for snow and ice sports.

The first Olympic bobsledders competed on open metal sleds. The basics have not changed, but modern racers sit within a **streamlined** pod that increases speed and protects in a crash. Tracks are specially built concrete chutes covered in ice, and speeds can reach up to 95 miles per hour (150 kilometers per hour).

Christel Cranz from Germany goes for gold at the 1936 Winter Olympic Games in Garmish-Partenkirchen, Germany. Ski technology has made Olympic skiing faster and safer.

Downhill skiing became part of the Olympics in 1936. A problem for early skiers was that if they fell over, the skis stayed attached to their feet. Broken legs were very common. Today's skiers have **bindings** that release their skis automatically. New inventions, including snowboards, have added new events to the Winter Olympics.

Wide, flexible snowboards are used for halfpipe tricks. The snowboard was invented in the 1960s.

Artificial snow

Technology can also be used to help the weather for the Winter Olympics. At one Vancouver venue in 2010, snow cannons were used to create **artificial** snow because not enough real snow had fallen. The cannons shoot water and air out of a nozzle into the cold air. This turns to ice before it hits the ground.

High-tech Paralympics

The **Paralympic** Games happen every four years, just after the Olympic Games. They are the biggest sporting event for athletes with disabilities. Cutting-edge **technology** enables many Paralympic athletes to compete at the Games, together with their own incredible skill and determination.

Technology has been adapted for sports at the Paralympics. One of these cyclists is the sighted "pilot," while the cyclist at the back is **visually impaired**.

Wheelchair sports

When wheelchair athletics first appeared at the Olympics in Tokyo, Japan, in 1964, the athletes did not use special wheelchairs. Now, wheelchairs used in Paralympic sports are very different from those you would see every day. They also vary from sport to sport. Athletics wheelchairs are designed to be very light for maximum speed. Wheelchair basketball players need to be able to move easily around the court.

Wheelchairs are not the only high-tech equipment at the Paralympics. Many athletes are **amputees**, who have to run or compete with **artificial** limbs, such as the "blade runner" Oscar Pistorius (see page 7).

Wheelchairs for athletics are designed to be light and have little **air resistance**. At longer distances, wheelchair athletes are quicker than able-bodied athletes.

Winning marathons

It is very difficult to compare the Olympics and Paralympics. Outside the Olympics, wheelchair athletes often race in **marathons** alongside runners. Amazing upper body strength means that wheelchair athletes can complete the 26-mile course more quickly than the runners.

Catching the Cheaters

Some high-tech developments are not good. Some athletes try to cheat by using **drugs** that improve their performance, and this is a big problem for the Olympics.

Drugs are nothing new for the Olympics. The winner of the 1904 **marathon** used poisonous strychnine to revive himself during the race. It was amazing he finished at all! The drugs some modern athletes use are designed to increase strength or give other benefits. Some drugs can be hidden by other substances to avoid detection in tests.

After effects

In 1988 Ben Johnson, the winner of the 100 meters, was found to have used drugs. Since then other sprinters have tested positive, too. Many other sports, such as weightlifting and gymnastics, have been affected. Athletes who use drugs cheat other athletes out of medals they should have won. There can also be serious long-term health problems linked to drugs.

Testing for drugs

Most Olympic medalists are now tested for drugs. Athletes provide a sample of urine, which is divided into two separate bottles for the "A" and "B" sample. The "A" sample is tested for drugs and, if anything is found, the athlete is told, and the "B" sample is tested to make sure. Athletes who are caught using drugs are banned and lose any medals or records they have won.

Ben Johnson's positive drug test made many people realize how big a problem drugs were for the Olympics.

The Future

Technology changes fast. It can be difficult to predict what will happen next. Many of the high-tech changes in this book have helped the Olympics. Athletes are more highly trained and eat better than ever before. New safety equipment prevents injuries, and timing and measuring equipment captures new world records.

However, not all technology is good. **Drugs** have tempted many athletes to cheat their fellow competitors. Less seriously, body suits that gave some swimmers a great advantage have been banned from the Olympics.

The Olympics and the media

One of the reasons why the Olympic Games are such a huge event is due to technology. People who wanted to know what was happening at the Athens Games of 1896 would have to wait days or weeks to read about it in the newspapers. The London 2012 Olympic Games will be beamed instantly to a massive television and online audience around the world. Technology means we can't miss the Olympics!

Limits of technology

The **Olympic Movement** aims to make sure the Games are about one athlete competing against another, not about who has the best technology. Technology has its place in the Olympics as long as the athletes, and not their clothing or equipment, are winning the gold medals.

The mass media makes an Olympic champion into an instant hero. A century ago, most people would not have known what the Olympic champion looked like.

Olympic Records–Now and Then

Event	Oldest Olympic record (men)	Current Olympic record (men)	Oldest Olympic record (women)	Current Olympic record (women)	Changes in technology
100 meters	12 seconds Thomas Burke, USA, 1896	9.69 seconds Usain Bolt, Jamaica, 2008	12.2 seconds Elizabeth Robinson, USA, 1928	10.62 seconds Florence Griffith-Joyner, USA, 1988	*Better training and diet. Changes in track and running shoes.*
Marathon	2 hours, 58 minutes, 50 seconds Spiridon Louis, Greece, 1896	2 hours, 6 minutes, 32 seconds Samuel Wanjiru, Kenya, 2008	2 hours, 24 minutes, 52 seconds Joan Benoit, USA, 1984	2 hours, 23 minutes, 14 seconds Naoko Takahashi, Japan, 2000	*Better training and diet*
High jump	1.81 meters Ellery Clark, USA, 1896	2.39 meters Charles Austin, USA, 1996	1.59 meters Ethel Catherwood, Canada, 1928	2.06 meters Yelena Slesarenko, Russia, 2004	*New technique— "Fosbury Flop"—made possible by softer landing mat*

Event	Oldest Olympic record (men)	Current Olympic record (men)	Oldest Olympic record (women)	Current Olympic record (women)	Changes in technology
Pole vault	**3.30 meters** William Welles Hoyt, USA, 1896	**5.96 meters** Steve Hooker, Australia, 2008	**4.60 meters** Stacy Dragila, USA, 2000	**5.05 meters** Yelena Isinbaeva, Russia, 2008	*Stronger and more flexible poles*
Javelin	**54.83 meters** Eric Lemming, Sweden, 1908	**94.58 meters** Miklos Nemeth, Hungary, 1976	**43.68 meters** Mildred "Babe" Didrikson, USA, 1932	**74.68 meters** Petra Felke, East Germany, 1988	*Improved fitness and technique. Javelin design changed to reduce throws (1986 for men, 1999 for women).*
Track cycling individual pursuit (4,000 meters for men, 3,000 meters for women)	**5 minutes, 4.75 seconds** Jiří Daler, Czechoslovakia, 1964	**4 minutes, 15.03 seconds** Bradley Wiggins, UK, 2008	**3 minutes, 41.75 seconds** Petra Rossner, Germany, 1992	**3 minutes, 24.54 seconds** Sarah Ulmer, New Zealand, 2004	*Lighter and more* **streamlined** *bikes including* **carbon fiber** *frames and solid wheels*
Swimming 100-meter freestyle	**1 minute, 22.2 seconds** Arnold Guttmann, Hungary, 1896	**47.05 seconds** Eamon Sullivan, Australia, 2008	**1 minute, 22.2 seconds** Sarah "Fanny" Durack, Australia, 1912	**53.12 seconds** Britta Steffen, Germany, 2008	*Better diet and training. Improved clothing including body suits at Beijing Olympics.*

Glossary

agile able to move easily and quickly

air resistance force that stops air from flowing smoothly over something

amputee someone who has lost one or more of their arms or legs

ancient Olympics Olympic Games held at Olympia in ancient Greece, beginning in 776 BCE

artificial not natural, made by people

binding in skiing, fixing between a ski boot and the ski

calorie unit of energy. All food contains calories.

carbohydrate substance in food that produces energy. Foods such as bread, rice, and pasta contain a lot of carbohydrates

carbon fiber light, but very strong, material used in a lot of high-tech sporting equipment

drug substance that affects the way your body or mind works. Using drugs can give some athletes an unfair advantage, but damages their health.

fiberglass plastic that contains fibers of glass to make it stronger

gears system on a car or bicycle that affects how fast the wheels will turn when force is applied, such as by pushing pedals. Bicycles use a low gear for going uphill and a high gear for going downhill and going faster.

marathon long running race held over 26.2 miles (42.2 kilometers)

Olympic Movement all the people involved in the Olympic Games, including the International Olympic Committee, Olympic officials from each country, and each Olympic sport

Paralympics games for athletes with a disability, held after the Olympic Games in the same place

podium raised platform

protein substance contained in food that helps the body to repair itself and grow new cells. Meat, fish, and dairy products contain a lot of protein.

stadium large arena for sporting events. The Olympic stadium is used for athletic events and the opening and closing ceremonies.

starting block device athletes use to steady themselves at the start of a race

streamlined designed to reduce air or water resistance

suspension system of springs that absorb shocks to make riding a mountain bike, or other vehicle, smoother

technology something developed using scientific or technical principles, from fabrics used in clothing to complex electronic gadgets

visually impaired disability affecting the sight, such as total loss of sight

Find Out More

Books

Brasch, Nicolas. *Sports and Sporting Equipment.* Mankato, MN: Smart Apple Media, 2011.

De Winter, James. *Secrets of Sport: The Technology that Makes Champions.* Mankato: Fact Finders, 2009.

Fridell, Ron. *Sports Technology.* Minneapolis, MN: Lerner Classroom, 2008.

Johnson, Robin. *Paralympic Sports Events.* New York: Crabtree Publishing, 2009.

Websites

oscarpistorius.com
Visit the official website of Oscar Pistorius to learn more about the Paralympic athlete's inspirational achievements.

www.design-technology.org
This website covers a lot of design and technology topics, including a section on sports shoes.

www.exploratorium.edu/explore/staff_picks/sports_science
This science museum website includes a section on the science behind different sports.

www.london2012.com
The website of the London 2012 Games includes details of venues and preparations for the Games, as well as information about Olympic sports.

www.olympic.org
The official website of the International Olympic Committee includes facts and statistics about every Olympic Games and medal winner.

Index